AR PTS: 1.0

Rich & Poor in Ancient Egypt

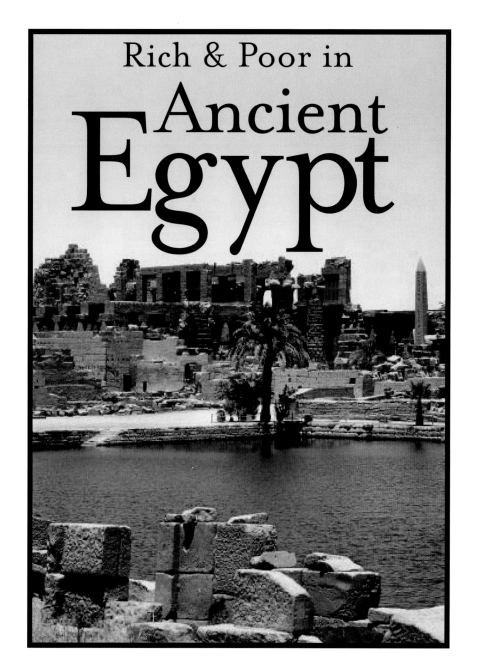

CLARE HIBBERT

Smart Apple Media

First published in 2005 by Franklin Watts
96 Leonard Street, London EC2A 4XD

Franklin Watts Australia
Level 17/207 Kent Street, Sydney NSW 2000

Produced by Arcturus Publishing Ltd.
26/27 Bickels Yard, 151–153 Bermondsey Street, London SE1 3HA

Series concept: Alex Woolf
Editor: Alex Woolf
Designer: Tim Mayer
Illustrator: Adam Hook
Picture researcher: Glass Onion Pictures

Picture Credits:
Front cover:
Art Archive: 4 (Egyptian Museum, Cairo / Dagli Orti), 6 (Egyptian Museum, Cairo / Dagli Orti),
7 (Dagli Orti), 8 (Musée du Louvre, Paris / Dagli Orti), 9 (Ragab Papyrus Institute, Cairo / Dagli Orti),
11 (Musée du Louvre, Paris / Dagli Orti), 12 (Egyptian Museum, Cairo / Dagli Orti [A]), 13 (Egyptian
Museum, Turin / Dagli Orti), 14 (Musée du Louvre, Paris / Dagli Orti), 15 (Carthage Museum / Dagli
Orti [A]), 18 (Egyptian Museum, Cairo / Dagli Orti [A]), 19 (Musée du Louvre, Paris / Dagli Orti),
20 (British Museum, London / Jacqueline Hyde), 21 (British Museum, London / Dagli Orti [A]),
22 (Egyptian Museum, Cairo / Dagli Orti), 24 (Dagli Orti), 25 (Musée du Louvre, Paris / Dagli Orti),
28 (Pharaonic Village, Cairo / Dagli Orti), 29 (British Museum, London / Jacqueline Hyde).
Bridgeman Art Library: 27 (British Museum, London).
British Museum: 17

Published in the United States by Smart Apple Media
2140 Howard Drive West, North Mankato, Minnesota 56003

Library of Congress Cataloging-in-Publication Data

Hibbert, Clare, 1970–
Ancient Egypt / by Clare Hibbert.
p. cm. — (Rich and poor in)
Includes index.
ISBN 1-58340-720-0
1. Egypt—Civilization—To 332 B.C.—Juvenile literature. I. Title. II. Series.

DT61.H47 2005
932'.01—dc22   2004062584

2 4 6 8 9 7 5 3 1

✦ CONTENTS ✦

RICH AND POOR 4

HOUSES AND HOMES 6

FAMILY LIFE 8

CLOTHING, JEWELRY, AND MAKEUP 10

FOOD 12

HEALTH AND MEDICINE 14

CHILDHOOD AND EDUCATION 16

WORK 18

LEISURE AND ENTERTAINMENT 20

TRANSPORTATION 22

RELIGION 24

DEATH AND MUMMIES 26

DEATH AND TOMBS 28

TIMELINE AND
FURTHER INFORMATION 30

GLOSSARY 31

INDEX 32

High Society

The richest person in ancient Egypt was the ruler, or pharaoh. Almost every pharaoh was a man, although there were a few female pharaohs. The pharaoh ruled over the "Two Lands" of Upper Egypt and Lower Egypt and was thought to be a god on earth. He lived in the royal palace.

❈ NOBLES AND PRIESTS ❈

After the pharaoh and his family, the next level of society was the nobility. Noblemen and noblewomen were wealthy landowners. The produce from their lands made them very rich and paid for a life of luxury.

The chief priests, who were in charge of the temples, were also rich.

Egypt's wealthy middle class was made up of scribes, architects, engineers, and doctors. Highly skilled craftspeople such as painters and jewelers could also be very well-off.

Pharaoh Thutmose III reigned from 1479 to 1425 B.C.. The cobra at the front of his headdress is a sign of the sun god, Re.

THE KING OF EGYPT

Here is a description of the pharaoh: "He is Re [the sun god], by whose rays one sees, for he is one who illuminates the Two Lands more than the sun disk. He is one who makes [the land] green, even more than a high inundation: he has filled the Two Lands with victory and life."
From the Sehetepibre Stele (1900s B.C.)

Low Life

Most people in Egypt were poor. Ordinary priests and craftspeople were not exactly poor, but they certainly were not rich. They worked hard and lived simply.

At the bottom of society were the enormous numbers of peasants and unskilled workers. They worked the fields to produce food for everyone and built and maintained the kingdom. They put in long hours of backbreaking work and usually died young.

Life was not much better for the men who served in the army and navy. Dancers, acrobats, and servants had difficult lives as well.

A servant brings food. In his right hand, he carries a pair of papyrus fans, which he will use to cool his master.

❧ SLAVERY ❧

Some servants were slaves. Most slaves in ancient Egypt were foreign prisoners of war. Some slaves did dangerous jobs such as mining or quarrying in the desert. Those who worked as domestic servants were the lucky ones.

Mud Mansions

This model of a house dates to the 1300s or 1400s B.C. A row of decorative stone columns stands at one end of the garden.

Although the Egyptians used stone for their great temples and tombs, all houses were built from mud bricks—even the pharaoh's palace.

Inside a rich person's home, the walls were decorated with colorful paintings or inlaid with semiprecious stones. Although they had little furniture, what they did have was beautifully carved. Beds often had wooden legs shaped like animals. There were tables, chairs, and chests, some of which were decorated with ebony and ivory.

❈ TOWN AND COUNTRY ❈

The pharaoh and nobility lived in cities such as Memphis and Thebes. Most nobles lived in tall town houses with many rooms. Some houses had a courtyard; all had a roof porch.

Even for the rich, city life could be cramped. Many also owned a country estate where they could keep an eye on the harvest. These estates had enough space for kitchen gardens and ponds.

Cramped Quarters

A Country Villa

These wise words come from a priest named 'Onchsheshonoqy, who lived in the 600s or 500s B.C.: "He who loves his house so as to dwell in it warms it to its beams. He who hates it builds it and then mortgages it."

From *The Instruction of 'Onchsheshonoqy*

The poor lived in simple mud brick houses within sprawling towns and villages. The houses were usually built on piles of garbage or on top of the ruins of older houses. Inside, the house had a few rooms, with areas for sleeping, eating, and praying.

Kitchens were usually outside because of the risk of fire. In summer, many people chose to sleep on the cool, breezy roof, rather than inside the sun-baked house. Poor families had just a few, very plain items of furniture in their homes, including stools, headrests, and storage chests.

❧ BARRACKS ❧

Special houses were built for the massive teams of laborers working on big projects such as temples, pyramids, or tomb complexes. Their small, barracks-style housing units were really just places to sleep. The workers ate together in a central canteen and bathed by the river.

Ruins of the huge housing complex at Deir el Medina. The builders and craftspeople who created the tombs in the Valley of the Kings lived here.

For Richer . . .

Egyptians married young, usually to a partner chosen by their parents. In the richest families, couples often married within the same family—some pharaohs even married their sisters. The couple signed a marriage contract that gave each partner equal rights over any property.

The woman's job was to stay at home, run the household, and raise the children. The mother chose her child's name. Children were breastfed for as long as three years, but rich women might pay a wet nurse to feed their children for them.

❖ CHILDCARE ❖

Children were very important, because when they grew up, they could look after their parents and give them a proper burial. Most couples had five children, and people who could not have children often adopted.

Pharaoh Akhenaten affectionately holds hands with his wife, Nefertiti. Akhenaten ruled from 1352 to 1336 B.C.

. . . For Poorer

Egyptian women gave birth in an upright position. Here, a mother kneels as a midwife delivers her baby. Other pictures show women using a low birthing stool for support.

Like the rich, the poor generally married within their own class. Most marriages were arranged, but some couples married for love. Poor people did not usually sign a marriage contract—partly because they could not afford to pay a scribe to draw one up and partly because they did not own much property to share between them.

As in rich marriages, there was no official wedding ceremony. The marriage began when the bride and groom set up a home together. However, even the poorest couples probably threw a party to celebrate.

⊲ GIVING BIRTH ⊳

Some women had as many as 15 children, but childbirth was dangerous. Roughly a third of all babies died, as did many mothers. Poor women could not afford to pay professional midwives. They usually gave birth at home, with a couple of neighboring women there to help.

HOW TO TREAT A WIFE

The scribe Ani advises his son how to keep a happy household: "Do not control your wife in her house when you know she is efficient. Do not say to her 'Where is it? Get it!' when she has put it in the right place. Let your eye observe in silence. Then you recognize her skill, it is joy when your hand is with her. . . ."

From *Instructions of Ani*

9

Colorful Collars

The rich wore finely woven linen, made into long, flowing dresses for women and pleated kilts for men. Sometimes men wore a woolen cape, too. Silk came late to Egypt, but the female pharaoh Cleopatra (51–30 B.C.) wore silk dresses.

Clothes were bleached white, but people wore colorful beaded collars. The rich also liked gold jewelry set with semiprecious stones or faience (a kind of ceramic).

Wealthy women adorned themselves with colorful gemstones: blue lapis lazuli, purple amethyst, red carnelian, and green feldspar.

A PRINCE'S GIFTS TO THE PHARAOH

"... armlets, gold bracelets, necklaces, collars inlaid with gemstones, amulets of every limb, garland crowns for the head, rings for the ears, every royal adornment. ... All of these I have presented in the royal presence, and clothing of royal linen by the thousands, being all the best of my weaving workshop."

From the Piye Victory Stele

❖ HAIR AND MAKEUP ❖

Both men and women rubbed scented oils into their skin and wore makeup. They used black kohl and green malachite for their eyes and also wore blush and lipstick.

Most people shaved their heads and wore wigs of plaited human hair. Boys—and some girls—kept one long lock of hair, known as the "sidelock of youth." Men stayed clean-shaven, but the pharaoh wore a ceremonial beard as a sign of kingship.

Coarse Cloth

The poor wore coarse, homespun linen. Linen came from the flax plant, one of Egypt's chief crops. The rough material was cut into simple loincloths for men and dresses for women. Women made the clothes, but men went down to the river to wash them—because of the danger of crocodiles! Servants wore finer clothes, given to them by their masters and mistresses.

✑ INEXPENSIVE JEWELS ✑

The poor liked jewelry and wore necklaces, earrings, and rings made of shells or beaten copper. They rubbed cheap castor oil into their skin. It didn't smell good, but it kept their skin soft.

Many of the poor shaved their heads, just like the rich. This kept them cool and prevented head lice. Some women grew their hair to sell for wigs.

Most poor Egyptians went barefoot, but some servants wore simple sandals woven from papyrus reeds.

Fine Feasts

Meat was a luxury that only the rich could afford. They ate beef, mutton, goat, goose, and duck. They also feasted on game animals, including antelope, ibex, gazelle, deer, ostrich, and hare. Roast meats were served at sumptuous banquets.

Many of the dishes were flavored with expensive herbs and spices such as coriander, aniseed, or cinnamon.

The rich also enjoyed many different cakes, cookies, and breads. The best bakers crafted dough into amazing shapes, even making cakes that looked like crocodiles.

✷ GARDEN PRODUCE ✷

In the towns, the rich had small courtyard gardens where they grew fresh vegetables and fruits, including grapes. Some grapes were eaten dried as raisins, but most were used for making wine, which was fermented in special jars. Before people drank it, the wine was sweetened with honey.

A husband and wife sit down to share a feast. The table is laden with meat, and there is a drinking cup of wine for each of them.

Bread and Beer

Bread was the staple food of the poor, although making it was hard work. First, the wheat grains were ground and sifted many times to make flour. This was made into a dough, then kneaded and baked. Sometimes the bread was flavored with herbs or sweet, sticky dates.

The poor ate the same vegetables as the rich, including lettuce, cucumbers, spinach, leeks, and onions. People also ate fruits such as melons, figs, dates, and pomegranates.

Most meals were washed down with beer, rather than water. The beer was made from soggy, half-cooked barley loaves, which were left to ferment in water.

⊲ GIFTS FROM THE RIVER ⊳

Beer and bread were gifts of the Nile, whose yearly flood spread rich mud over the fields and fertilized the crops. The river also supplied fish and small game birds such as cranes, ducks, and quail.

This tomb model shows a kitchen. On the left, servants grind barley and knead bread dough. In the center are barrels of fermenting beer.

TOO MUCH WINE

This is part of a story about Pharaoh Amasis (570–526 B.C.): "Pharaoh drank an extremely large quantity of wine because of the craving that he had for a vat of Egyptian wine. . . . Morning came, and Pharaoh was unable to raise himself. . . . Pharaoh said: 'I have a terrible hangover. It isn't [in my] power to do any work at all.'"

From *The Tale of Amasis and the Skipper*

Costly Care

This 3,500-year-old fragment of papyrus contains instructions for making a medicine. The ingredients include honey, fat, and galena (poisonous lead sulphide).

W hen they were sick, the rich visited doctors—and some of them *were* doctors. Medicine was such a well-respected profession that only people from high-class families could enter it. The very first physician, Imhotep (c. 2650 B.C.), was later worshipped as the god of medicine.

Egyptian doctors were taught at special schools, where they studied ancient medical texts. Medical students did not practice on real patients, but they were able to examine dead bodies.

✷ TREATING THE SICK ✷

Egyptian doctors used plants with healing properties and spread honey, a known antiseptic, on open wounds. They also knew how to stitch up wounds, mend fractures, and diagnose pregnancy.

DOCTOR'S NOTES

These notes were jotted down around 1800 B.C.: "The patient . . . feels a heavy, hot, and inflamed body. He complains of being unable to tolerate his clothes and feels they do not warm him. He feels thirsty during the night. His saliva has the taste of unripe fruits. His muscles pain him as if he walked for a long distance."
From the Berlin Papyrus

Almost all doctors specialized in treating just one particular part of the body, such as the eyes, teeth, or abdomen. The pharaoh had a whole army of court physicians, ready to treat his every ailment.

Homemade Healing

The very poor could not afford doctors. If they fell ill, they saved up to buy medicines from a chemist or relied on homemade remedies. Most medicines contained herbs or other plant extracts. Thyme, for example, was taken for general pain relief, while dill relieved constipation.

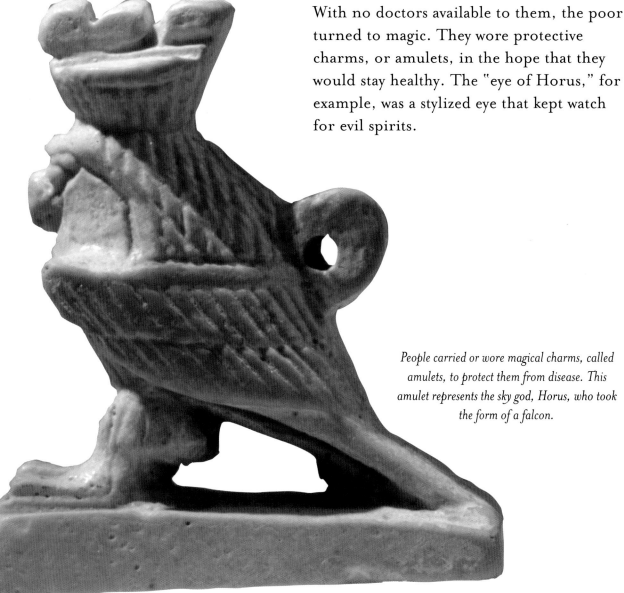

People carried or wore magical charms, called amulets, to protect them from disease. This amulet represents the sky god, Horus, who took the form of a falcon.

⊰ COMMON COMPLAINTS ⊱

Disease spread quickly among the poor because they lived so close together. There were outbreaks of malaria, smallpox, tuberculosis, and cholera. People also suffered injuries at work or developed lung diseases from breathing in too much sand.

With no doctors available to them, the poor turned to magic. They wore protective charms, or amulets, in the hope that they would stay healthy. The "eye of Horus," for example, was a stylized eye that kept watch for evil spirits.

Privileged Pupils

Scribes were the best-educated ancient Egyptians. Boys who were going to become scribes began school at the age of five. They had to copy rows of hieroglyphs and learn long passages of text by heart.

Princes and princesses also learned reading, writing, and math, but they did not attend school. They studied with private tutors.

Scribes wrote on a kind of paper made from papyrus reeds. Bundles of reed stems were tied together to make a paintbrush. This was dipped in ink made from soot or red earth.

❈ WORK AND PLAY ❈

Most well-off boys and girls did not have any schooling. Instead, their parents taught them how to manage an estate or run a household. Some boys completed apprenticeships in order to prepare for a career such as medicine, architecture, or the priesthood.

When they were not busy learning, rich children enjoyed swimming, riding horses, and archery. They had toys, including rag dolls and wooden animals with moving parts. In the richest families, children kept pets—cats, dogs, or even monkeys.

ADVICE TO A YOUNG SCRIBE

"O scribe, do not be idle, do not be idle, or you shall be curbed straightaway. Do not give your heart to pleasures, or you shall fail. Write with your hand, recite with your mouth, and converse with those more knowledgeable than you."
From the Papyrus Anastasi

Child Labor

Poor children did not need to read or write, and their parents could not afford to send them to school. Both boys and girls were expected to help their parents and look after younger brothers and sisters.

Most children learned to do their parents' jobs. Peasants' children took part in the sowing and harvesting. They even acted as human scarecrows to keep the birds off the crops. Servants' children ran errands or helped prepare food. Sons of tomb builders were sometimes lucky enough to win a place on one of the building crews, where they could do odd jobs and learn the skills of the craft.

These simple spinning tops were made of cheap, molded quartz crystals. A child could start the top spinning by hand or wind papyrus twine around it and then pull.

✥ FUN TIMES ✥

Not even poor children were expected to work until they were five. Before then, they played with simple toys such as balls and dolls and made up exciting games, such as pretend battles.

Top Jobs

Everyone worked in ancient Egypt—
even the pharaoh! Since he was
thought to be a god on earth, he
had to take part in special ceremonies
throughout the year. He also had to run
the country, meet foreign officials,
and rule over his generals.

The best-paid jobs in the land
were for high priests, officials,
and scribes. There were many
official jobs in ancient Egypt,
such as collecting taxes for
the pharaoh or judging
criminals. These jobs
were almost always held by noblemen,
although there were a few women scribes
and at least one woman judge.

❈ BEAUTIFUL THINGS ❈
Not all craftspeople were rich, but the
most skillful were paid well for their
work. They painted beautiful
murals on the walls of temples and
tombs or designed stunning
jewelry using semiprecious
stones. Some of them made
fine pottery; others carved
elegant furniture.

*Scribes were always in demand
and earned good wages. They
were employed to record
court judgements or yields
from the fields. This
statue of a scribe dates to
around 2400 B.C.*

Tough Toil

This wall painting shows workers in the fields. They use curved knives called sickles to harvest the crop.

The poor did much more physical work than the rich. The most difficult work was *corvée*, or national service. This was when the pharaoh called on everyone in the land—except his officials—to work on a project such as building a temple, farming, or repairing an irrigation system. Richer people could buy their way out of doing national service, so in the end, all of the backbreaking work fell on the poor.

❧ HARD LABOR ❧

By far, the largest group of poor workers were the peasant laborers. The land they cultivated usually belonged to the pharaoh or a nobleman. Peasants worked long hours but earned scarcely enough to live on.

Another tough job was serving in the army. Soldiers were expected to walk long distances on short rations and were beaten if they did not keep up.

A SOLDIER'S LIFE

"His rations and his water are upon his shoulder like the load of a donkey, while his neck has been made a backbone like that of a donkey. The vertebrae of his back are broken, while he drinks of foul water. He stops work [only] to keep watch."

From the Papyrus Anastasi

Rich Revels

The rich enjoyed throwing lavish banquets, and the pharaoh's feasts were the most extravagant of all. Besides eating and drinking, guests were entertained. Dancing girls performed acrobatic routines. Musicians played flutes, harps, and cymbals.

✖ FAVORITE PASTIMES ✖

In their spare time, Egyptian noblemen liked to go hunting with dogs, either at the marshy edges of the Nile or out in the desert. They used various weapons, including spears, arrows, throwing sticks, and nets.

The board game of *senet* was popular with everyone in Egypt. The rich owned beautiful senet sets made of costly ebony and ivory or inlaid with semiprecious stones.

Senet was a game for two players. Each started with seven pieces and tried to be first to take all of his or her pieces off the board. The players threw sticks to move around the squares.

HUNTING BY THE NILE

Bird trapping and fishing in the marshes by the river:

"A happy day when we go down to the marsh, that we may snare birds and catch many fish in the waters. . . . a happy day on which we give to everybody and the marsh goddess is propitious. We shall trap birds and shall light a brazier to Sobek [the crocodile god]."

From *The Pleasures of Fishing and Fowling*

Songs and Stories

Storytelling did not cost anything and was the main way that ordinary people relaxed in the evenings after work. Some stories recounted adventures of heroes; others told myths about the gods, which sometimes explained natural events.

One tale, for example, told how the yearly flooding of the Nile came from the tears of the goddess Isis. She was said to be weeping to mark the anniversary of her husband Osiris's death.

◁ Music and Dance ◁

The poor played simple percussion instruments, such as rhythm sticks and drums, to beat time while they worked. They also played music for relaxation. Love songs were popular, as were ballads about heroes or pharaohs.

Not all dancing and music making was for pleasure. Poor dancers and musicians performed at funerals as professional mourners, in addition to entertaining the rich at their banquets.

This wall painting from around 1350 B.C. shows entertainers at a feast. The musicians have cones of perfumed grease on their heads.

Traveling in Style

On land, the very richest people used one-man horse-drawn chariots to move from place to place. Chariots were ideal for hunting trips or charging into battle, but horses were rare. Most rich people traveled in a litter—a chair on poles carried by servants.

✖ THE MIGHTY NILE ✖

All of the towns and cities in Egypt grew up along the banks of the River Nile, so people usually traveled by boat, which kept them cool. The rich had their own private boats made of reeds or wood. The finest boats, including the pharaoh's royal barge, were built of cedarwood imported from Lebanon. Boats sailed south because the wind always blew in that direction. When traveling north, they relied on a team of oarsmen.

Pharaoh Tutankhamun, who reigned from 1332 to 1322 B.C., rides into battle against the Syrians in a horse-drawn war chariot. The scene decorates a wooden chest found in Tutankhamun's tomb.

Boats and Beasts

Even the poor traveled by boat. They built simple rafts or small fishing boats from papyrus reeds. These boats did not offer much protection against the wild crocodiles and hippopotamuses of the Nile.

There were also large passenger ferries and cargo barges. These carried laborers and heavy supplies to the sites of the pyramids, tomb complexes, and temples.

⊰ LAND TRAVEL ⊱

When on land, the poor walked. Some people wore reed sandals to protect their feet on hot or stony ground, but most went barefoot. They used sturdy cattle and donkeys to help carry supplies such as food or wine.

The poor also had to transport enormous weights, such as the 2.75-ton (2.5 t) stone blocks used to build the pyramids. It is likely that these blocks were moved from the riverbank up to the building site using strong papyrus ropes—and the pulling power of hundreds of men.

A LOVE SONG

"I am sailing downstream on the ferry, [guided] by the hand of the helmsman, with my bundle of reeds on my shoulder. I am bound for [Memphis], and I shall say to Ptah [the creator], the Lord of Ma'at [universal order], 'Grant me my beloved this night.'"

From the Love Songs of Papyrus Harris 500

Fishing boats such as this one did not offer much defense against a crocodile attack.
They were simple rowboats made from tightly tied bundles of reeds.

Sacred Secrets

The most important religious rites were performed by the pharaoh or on his behalf by priests and priestesses. The pharaoh was thought to be the son of the sun god, Re. By carrying out special ceremonies, he helped to ensure a good harvest or the safety of his people.

❖ HOUSES OF THE GODS ❖

Priests and priestesses also worshipped on behalf of the whole population. They chanted prayers and spells, made music using a sacred rattle called a sistrum, and performed sacred dances. They also made daily offerings of food, wine, and perfumed oils to the gods.

Priests and priestesses lived in the temple complexes built at Abydos, Thebes (Luxor), and nearby Karnak. Each temple was dedicated to a particular god, such as Re, Osiris (king of the dead), Thoth (god of knowledge), or Isis (goddess of love). Ordinary people were not allowed to go into the temples.

A PHARAOH'S RELIGIOUS DUTIES

"Perform the monthly priestly service, don white sandals; enrich the temple, be discreet concerning the mysteries; enter into the holy place, eat bread in the house of the god; replenish the offerings, multiply the sacrificial loaves; increase the daily offerings. . . ."
From the Teaching for King Merykara
(c. 2025–1700 B.C.)

Ruins of the Temple of Amun at Karnak. Amun was originally associated only with the city of Thebes but later became Egypt's supreme god.

Festivals and Shrines

Poor and rich alike gathered to watch the many religious festivals that took place throughout the year. During the festival of Opet, held at Thebes, people lined the banks of the Nile while statues of the gods were carried along the river.

People also visited small shrines where they could pray to a god and make offerings. If they could afford it, people paid to have their prayer engraved onto a small stone tablet called a stele. Some stelae included a picture of an ear to make sure the god would hear the prayer.

☙ HOUSEHOLD GODS ❧

Most people had miniature shrines in their houses—small alcoves where they kept a statue of a god. Popular household deities included Taweret, the hippopotamus goddess of fertility and childbirth, and the dwarf god Bes, protector of households and bringer of domestic happiness.

Most Egyptian deities took the form of an animal. Taweret, goddess of childbirth, was seen as a hippopotamus. Female hippos are known for fiercely defending their offspring.

Mummy Making

All ancient Egyptians believed that when they died they needed their physical body for the afterlife. Rich people had their bodies wrapped and preserved as mummies.

Mummification was a long, complicated process that took 70 days. Specially trained embalmers washed the body in scented oil and then carefully removed the organs—all except the heart. Next, they left the body in natron salt for 40 days to dry it out.

✖ WRAPPING UP ✖

After packing the body with linen or sawdust and oiling the skin, the embalmers bandaged the mummy from head to toe. They put magic charms between the bandages. As they worked, a priest chanted special prayers. He wore a mask of Anubis, the jackal-headed god of embalming.

Finally, a death mask was placed over the mummy's head, and the body was placed in a wooden coffin, which was sometimes placed inside another box called a sarcophagus.

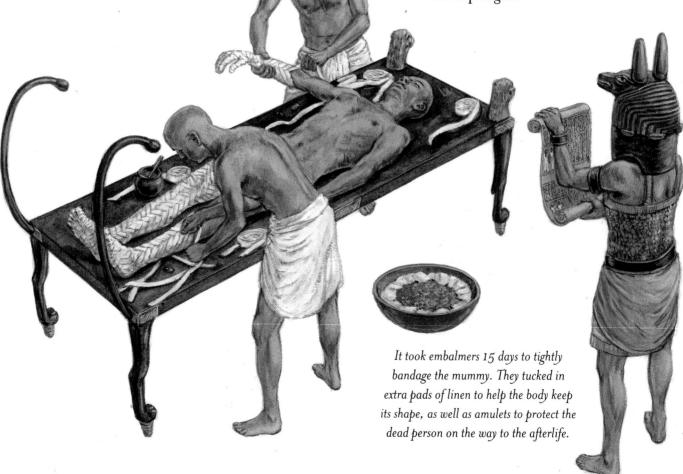

It took embalmers 15 days to tightly bandage the mummy. They tucked in extra pads of linen to help the body keep its shape, as well as amulets to protect the dead person on the way to the afterlife.

Common Graves

The attention and skills of embalmers and priests were far too expensive for the poor, although there were a few exceptions. Servants were sometimes made into mummies so that they could be buried with their master or mistress, ready to serve them again in the next life.

⊰ Fuss-Free Funerals ⊱

Most poor people were placed in simple coffins made of papyrus reeds or, sometimes, wood. The very poorest were not even buried in coffins. They were simply thrown into shallow pits dug on the edge of the desert. These bodies were often brilliantly preserved. The dry desert sand mummified them naturally. Some poor people's bodies are even better preserved than the mummies of the rich.

This man, buried with just a few possessions, was naturally preserved by the hot desert sand. Known as "Ginger," he lived around 3200 B.C.—before Egypt was ruled by the pharaohs.

How to Make a Mummy

"First, with the crooked iron tool, they draw out the brain through the nostrils . . . and after this, with a sharp stone of Ethiopia, they make a cut along the side and take out the whole contents of the belly, and when they have cleared out the cavity and cleansed it with palm wine, they cleanse it again with spices pounded up. . . ."

From Herodotus's *Histories*

Treasure-Filled Tombs

The mummified bodies of the rich were placed in a tomb, along with belongings for the afterlife. These included real clothing, jewels, furniture, and weapons, as well as models of larger items such as boats and chariots. People were even buried with clay models of food and drink. Paintings on the wall showed the person's house and family, in the hope that the same riches and happiness would be enjoyed in the afterlife.

✖ TOMB TYPES ✖

The most spectacular ancient Egyptian tombs are the pyramids—towering triangular tombs built for some of the early pharaohs. The Great Pyramid at Giza was designed to help point the pharaoh to the sky to join his father, the sun god.

Unfortunately, the pyramids were raided for the riches inside. Later, pharaohs and other rich people were buried in hidden underground tombs cut into the hard desert rock.

One of the rooms inside Tutankhamun's tomb. Among the many treasures are three gilded wooden couches, shaped as a lion, a cow, and a hippopotamus. At the far end, two statues guard the way into the main burial chamber.

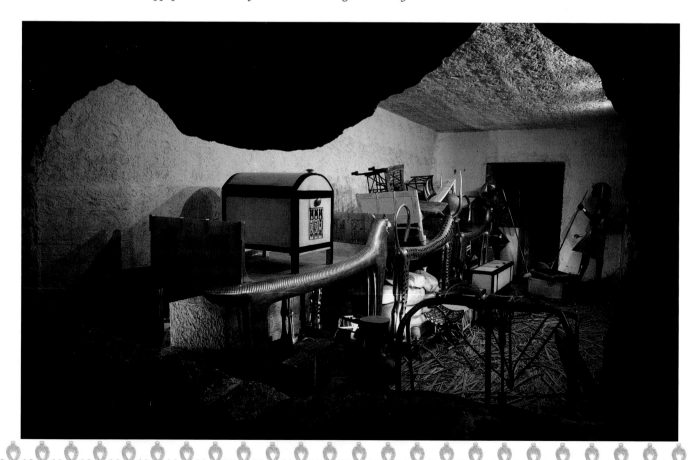

Heavenly Hopes

Poor people didn't have special tombs, but they did make sure that they were buried with a few possessions and some food. Like the rich, they believed their bodies would have to make a journey to the afterlife, the heavenly kingdom ruled by the god Osiris.

☙ JOURNEY TO OSIRIS'S KINGDOM ☙

First, the dead person had to ask a ferryman to carry him across a river. Then he had to go through seven carefully guarded gates. Atum, a creator god, and Hathor, the goddess of beauty, were there to help him, but there were also evil gods, snakes, and crocodiles to try to outwit him.

HOW TO ENTER THE AFTERLIFE

"A man should say this spell when pure and clean, dressed in clothing, shod in white sandals, painted with black eye paint, anointed with the finest myrrh oil, and having offered fresh meat, fowl, incense, bread, beer, and vegetables."

From the *Book of the Dead*

Next, the dead person had to face 42 judges before his heart was weighed in the Hall of Two Truths. If the dead person's heart was heavier than the feather of truth, he was devoured by a monster. If his heart was light, he was allowed into the afterlife.

The god Anubis leads a dead person to the afterlife, then weighs his heart against the feather of truth. To the right, the god Osiris sits on his throne.

B.C.

c. 7000   First farming settlements are established along the Nile.

4236   The first date in the ancient Egyptian calendar.

c. 3050   Upper and Lower Kingdoms of Egypt unite under one pharaoh, Narmer (Menes).

c. 3000   Hieroglyphic writing appears. City of Memphis is founded. Earliest mummy making.

c. 2700   Trade for jewels and cedarwood begins with Lebanon, Byblos, and Somalia.

c. 2650s   Worship of Re (the sun god) begins. Step pyramids are built at Saqqara.

c. 2575–   Pyramids and Sphinx are built at Giza.
c. 2465

c. 1850   Egyptians conquer Nubia to the south.

c. 1630   Asian invaders, the Hyksos, introduce the horse and chariot to Egypt.

c. 1550   Mummy making process is perfected.

c. 1510   Construction of Temple of Amun-Re at Karnak.

1504   Death of Thutmose I, the first pharaoh to be buried in the Valley of the Kings.

c. 1500   The world's oldest known medical text, the Ebers papyrus, is written.

c. 1380s   Worship of Amun (a creator god) stops. Worship of the sun-disk god, Aten, begins. Capital moves to el-Amarna.

1330s   The boy pharaoh, Tutankhamun, reestablishes worship of Amun. Royal court returns to Thebes and Memphis.

524–404   Persian kings rule over Egypt.

305–30   Greeks rule Egypt following Alexander the Great's invasion. Capital moves to Alexandria.

30   Egypt becomes a province of ancient Rome.

Further Reading

Harris, Geraldine, and Delia Pemberton. *Illustrated Encyclopedia of Ancient Egypt*. Lincolnwood, Ill.: Peter Bedrick Books, 1999.

Malam, John. *Mummies*. Boston: Kingfisher, 2003.

Millard, Anne. *The Story of the Nile*. New York: DK Publishing, 2003.

Walker, Jane. *100 Things You Should Know about Mummies*. Broomall, Pa.: Mason Crest Publishers, 2003.

Web sites

http://www.ancient-egypt.org

http://www.carnegieinstitute.org/cmnh/exhibits/egypt

http://www.pbs.org/wgbh/nova/pyramid

amulet A magical charm that protects the wearer.

anointed Rubbed with oil.

antiseptic A substance that kills bacteria and prevents infection.

apprenticeship Working with a master craftsman in order to learn his trade.

balm A soothing ointment.

barracks Soldiers' living quarters.

brazier A small, contained fire.

cholera A usually fatal bacterial infection of the small intestine, caused by dirty water. Victims suffer diarrhea, vomiting, and cramps.

cultivated Describes land that is being used for growing crops.

diagnose Identify a condition or disease.

domestic Connected to a household.

embalmer Someone who treats dead bodies so that they do not rot.

faience Colored, glazed ceramic.

ferment Turn into alcohol through the action of yeasts.

fertility The ability to produce offspring or crops.

gazelle A small, wild antelope found in northern Africa and southwest Asia.

helmsman The person who steers a boat.

hieroglyph A small picture or symbol. The Egyptians wrote using hieroglyphs. Each hieroglyph might stand for a sound or a whole word.

ibex A wild mountain goat found in Europe, north Africa, and Asia.

incense Resin, or plant sap, that gives off sweet-smelling fumes when it is burned.

inflamed Hot and swollen.

inundation Flood.

irrigation The process of bringing a supply of water to a dry area in order to help crops grow.

jackal A wild dog found in Africa and Asia.

kohl Black powder used as eye makeup.

loincloth A long piece of cloth that wraps between the legs and ties at the waist, worn as a basic garment or undergarment.

malachite A green mineral.

malaria A fever passed on to humans by mosquito bites.

mortgage Take out a loan of money, using one's house as security—that is, agreeing to hand over the house if the loan repayments cannot be met.

mural A wall painting.

myrrh oil Highly prized, strong-smelling oil extracted from the bark of the Commiphora, or incense, tree.

natron A natural rock salt, used by embalmers to dry out bodies.

papyrus A reed that grows by the Nile. The Egyptians used it to make many useful things, including ropes, baskets, and a form of paper.

pleated Having many folds of cloth.

propitious Lucky or favorable.

sarcophagus A large stone box in which a coffin was placed.

smallpox A usually fatal viral infection, spread through the air. Victims suffer fever, chills, and aches, followed by itchy, pus-filled red spots.

snare Trap.

stele A piece of stone with writing on it.

stylized Not realistic; following a particular artistic "look."

tuberculosis A usually fatal bacterial infection of the lungs or of the bones and joints.

Two Lands Upper Egypt (the south of the country) and Lower Egypt (the north, where the Nile empties into the Mediterranean Sea). Originally two different kingdoms, the Two Lands were united by Pharaoh Menes around 2900 B.C.

vertebrae Sections of backbone.

⊹ INDEX ⊹

Page numbers in **bold** refer to illustrations.

afterlife 26, 28, 29, **29**
architects 4, 16
army 5, 19

banquets and feasts 12, **12**, 20, 21
boats 22, 23, 28

chariots 22, **22**, 28, 30
childbirth 9, 9
children 8, 10, 16–17
cities 6, 22, 24, 25, 30
  Alexandria 30
  el-Amarna 30
  Memphis 6, 30
  Thebes 6, 24, 25, 30
clothes 10–11, 14, 28, 29
courtyard gardens 6, **6**, 12
craftspeople 4, 5, 7, 18
criminals 18
crocodiles 11, 12, 20, 23, **23**, 29

dancing 5, 20, 21, **21**, 24
death and burial 8, 21, 26–29, 30
disease 15
doctors 4, 14, 15

education 16–17
entertainment 20–21

family life 8–9
farming 5, 13, 17, 19, **19**, 24, 30
festivals 25
food 5, 12–13, 23, 24, 28, 29
furniture 6, 7, 18, 28

gods and goddesses 4, 14, 15, 18, 20, 21, 24, 25, 26, 28, 29, 30
  Amun 30

Anubis 26, **29**
Aten 30
Atum 29
Bes 25
Hathor 29
Horus **15**
Imhotep 14
Isis 21, 24
Osiris 21, 24, 29, **29**
Re 4, 24, 28, 30
Tawaret 25, **25**
Thoth 24

hair 10, 11
health 14–15
hieroglyphs 16, 30, 31
hippopotamuses 23, 25, **25**, **28**
houses 6–7, 6, 7, 25
hunting 20, 22

irrigation 19, 31

jewelry 10, **10**, 11, 18, 28, 30
judges 18, 29

leisure 20–21
linen 10, 11, 26
litters 22

magic and spells 15, 24, 26
makeup 10, 29
marriage 8, 9
medicine 14–15, 16, 30
mining 5
mummies 26, 27, 30
music 20, 21, **21**, 24
myths 21

national service 19
Nile, the 13, 20, 21, 22, 23, 25
nobles 4, 6, 18, 19

paintings 6, 18
palaces 4
peasants 5, 17, 19
pharaohs 4, 6, 8, 10, 13, 14, 18, 19, 20, 21, 22, 24, 28, 30
  Akhenaten **8**
  Amasis 13
  Cleopatra 10
  Narmer 30
  Thutmose I 30
  Thutmose III **4**
  Tutankhamun **22**, 28, 30
priests 4, 5, 7, 16, 18, 24, 26
pyramids 7, 23, 28, 30

religion 24–25
religious ceremonies 18, 24

scribes 4, 9, 16, 16, 18, 18
senet 20, **20**
servants 5, **5**, 8, 11, **13**, 17, 22, 27
shoes 11, **11**, 23, 24, 29
shrines 25
slaves 5
stele 25, 31
storytelling 21

temples 4, 6, 7, 18, 19, 23, 24, **24**, 30
tombs 6, 7, 7, 17, 18, 23, 28–29, **28**
toys 16, 17, **17**
transportation 22–23

warfare 22, **22**
weapons 20, 28
women 4, 8, 9, 10, 11, 18
work 18–19